Editorial Project Manager
Dona Herweck Rice

Editor
Jennifer Overend Prior, M.Ed.

Editor-in-Chief
Sharon Coan, M.S. Ed.

Art Coordinator
Denice Adorno

Imaging
Alfred Lau

Product Manager
Phil Garcia

Publishers
Rachelle Cracchiolo, M.S. Ed.
Mary Dupuy Smith, M.S. Ed.

Student Writer's Notebook

Level 3

Author

Shelle Russell

Teacher Created Materials, Inc.
6421 Industry Way
Westminster, CA 92683
www.teachercreated.com
ISBN-0-7439-3559-4
©2001 Teacher Created Materials, Inc.
Reprinted, 2002, a
Made in U.S.A.

Student Writer's Notebook

A nonfiction reading & writing program • A nonfiction reading & writing program

Table of Contents

Student Writer's Notebook

A nonfiction reading & writing program • A nonfiction reading & writing program

Table of Contents (cont.)

About the Student Writer's Notebook

It will be useful for the students to have a manual for basic information and helpful tips. The pages of this section serve that purpose. Reproduce this section as a whole or by selecting those pages that fit your needs and distribute them to the students. The students can store their notebook pages in a three-ring binder or other secure folder that will allow them to look through the pages with ease. The students may use their notebooks to take notes as they learn about writing.

Writing Process

I. **Pre-writing** (planning)—It comes before writing. The writer thinks about ideas, asks questions, looks for ideas, or gathers information for research.

II. **Writing the First Draft**—The author writes down notes, ideas, or information he or she wants to share.

III. **Responding**—(optional) The author allows another student to read what has been written for comments or to offer suggestions.

IV. **Revising**—The author changes and improves his or her work by reorganizing sentences or paragraphs giving special attention to capitals, punctuation, quotation marks, clear thoughts, and organization.

V. **Editing**—Using the editing checklist, the author corrects and makes writing more clear. A final check is done for spelling, punctuation, and sentence structure.

VI. **Publishing**—The author makes a final, careful copy of his or her work.

VII. **Follow-up Illustrations**—The author adds desired illustrations to accompany the writing.

Student Writer's Notebook

A nonfiction reading & writing program • *A nonfiction reading & writing program*

Tips for Good Writing

The best writing is clear and easy to read. The most creative ideas will be lost if the writing is too complicated, fancy, or has too many adjectives or adverbs. Here are some tips:

- **The most important words are nouns and verbs.** Nouns and verbs are the words needed to write and speak a sentence. Use nouns and verbs that will tell a story or "paint a clear picture" for the reader. Use verbs that show action. For example, instead of saying:

The girl had a good time at the party.

say:

Sarah was joyful and enjoyed the party.

Sarah's name and the words joyful and enjoyed show a specific person and specific feelings. The sentence shows us a certain girl acting in a certain way.

- **Write every day.** Set a daily goal of fifty to 100 words. Make sure it is a goal you can reach. Write in a journal, a dairy, or whatever you wish, but write every day. When you write and rewrite, practice makes perfect.

- **Try to learn to type.** The computer can be your best friend when writing.

- **Keep a dictionary and a thesaurus near by and use them regularly.**

- **Rewrite! Rewrite! Rewrite!** Almost any sentence you write can be written in many different ways. Learn to rewrite so that you find the clearest way to say the things that you want to say.

- **Read your writing out loud.** Reading out loud helps you to know whether or not your writing makes sense. This is especially true if you read to family members, friends, or other people.

- **Read! Read! Read!** Read anything and everything you can, but especially read things written by good authors. Reading will give you a better ability to communicate clearly and further improve your writing skills.

More Tips for Good Writing

✔ When it is possible, it is always best to complete the full writing process at one time. The full writing process involves several drafts, brainstorming, asking someone else to criticize your writing, creating a final draft, and publishing your work.

✔ Keep track of editing marks or corrections that your teacher makes on your papers. Check for spelling mistakes and incomplete sentences. Add words you misspell often to your personal spelling list.

✔ Check to be sure you have labeled your paper completely with your name, date, title, and any other items required by your teacher.

✔ Reading often will help all areas of your writing—spelling, punctuation, grammar, and vocabulary.

✔ Good handwriting is very important. A neatly written answer usually receives a higher grade.

✔ At times you may feel that you do not have enough time to complete even the quick steps for writing. If this happens, quickly go through the step in your mind, if you do not have time to do it on the paper. Most importantly, proofread your answer.

✔ When your writing assignment asks a question, make sure to restate the question in your answer. This will help to make your answer clear. A restated question makes an excellent topic sentence for a paragraph.

  Example:

  Q: What is a nonfiction book report?

  A: A nonfiction book report is a report that tells you about a true story.

Glossary of Writing Terms

Edit: Make writing clear for the reader in two stages:

- revising—reordering, rewording, making ideas clear
- editing—spelling corrections, punctuation, grammar

Expository: This type of writing focuses on factual information about the reader, someone known or someone researched. This type of writing is different from narrative, because the author does not include feelings or emotions, only facts.

Focus: The clearness used by the author to share ideas, thoughts, and knowledge.

Structure: This involves organization, design, sequence of ideas, and construction of the writing. This is specific to the genre assigned. It also includes topic sentence, arranging, and sequencing.

Genre: This is a specific type of writing. Types of genre include: narrative, expositive, persuasive, biographical, autobiographical, cause-effect, problem-solution, first person, and story writing.

Narrative: There are two types of narrative writing. In the first, the author reflects and recounts a personal experience. In the second, the author reports and records actions of an event which was observed. Personal narratives reflect author's actions and reactions. Third person narratives tell about an event and describe those who participated in it.

Organization: The clear, logical way that ideas flow and the way that the ideas are organized in the paper.

Persuasive: There are two kinds of persuasive writing. In the first, the author takes a position and shares an argument. In the second, the author develops a problem and a solution to that problem.

Tools of the Writer's Trade

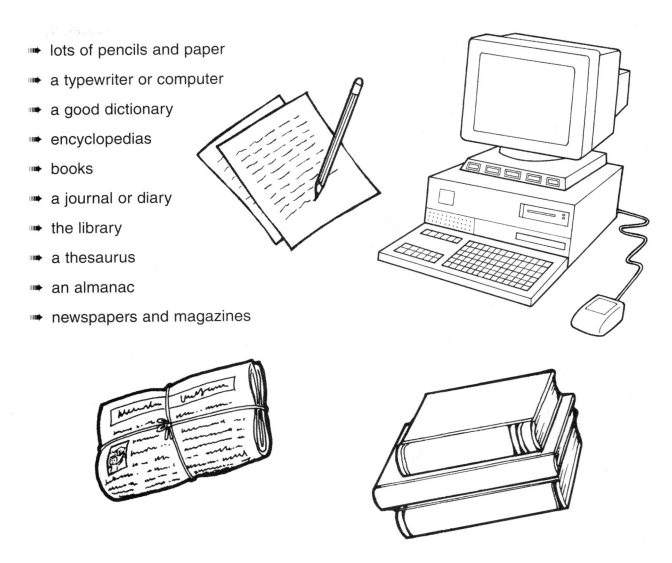

- lots of pencils and paper
- a typewriter or computer
- a good dictionary
- encyclopedias
- books
- a journal or diary
- the library
- a thesaurus
- an almanac
- newspapers and magazines

Using Writing Tools

1. Spend some time learning how to use one of the writer's tools listed above.

2. Write an article that tells how this tool can be useful to you when you are doing a writing assignment.

3. In your article, use examples to show how the writing tool can help you with your writing.

Parts of Speech

On each of the "Parts of Speech" pages, write a running list of words that fit each category. Use additional pages, as necessary.

Nouns	Pronouns
words that name a person, place, thing, or idea	words used in place of a noun

Parts of Speech *(cont.)*

Verbs	Adjectives
words that show action or a state of being (existence)	words that describe a noun or pronoun

Parts of Speech *(cont.)*

Adverbs

words that modify a verb, adjective, or other adverb

Prepositions

words that show how the object and another word are related

Parts of Speech *(cont.)*

Conjunctions	**Interjections**
words that connect other words	words used to show strong emotion

Conjugating Verbs

To *conjugate* a verb means to write it in each of its different tenses. A tense of a verb shows the time frame in which it takes place.

The tenses are:
- **present tense**—it is happening now or on a regular basis
- **past**—it has already happened
- **future**—it will happen

Example of the conjugation of a regular verb (to sail) in the first person singular (1):

> I sail. (present)
>
> I sailed. (past)
>
> I will sail. (future)

Example of the conjugation of an irregular verb (to swim) in the first person singular (1):

> I swim. (present)
>
> I swam. (past)
>
> I will swim. (future)

Chart of the principle conjugation parts of the 40 irregular verbs:

Present	Past	Past Participle	Present	Past	Past Participle
am/be	was/were	been	lie (recline)	lay	lain
begin	began	begun	ride	rode	ridden
bite	bit	bitten	ring	rang	rung
blow	blew	blown	rise	rose	risen
break	broke	broken	run	ran	run
bring	brought	brought	see	saw	seen
catch	caught	caught	shake	shook	shaken
come	came	come	shine (light)	shone	shone
do	did	done	shrink	shrank	shrunk
drink	drank	drunk	sing	sang/sung	sung
drive	drove	driven	sit	sat	sat
drown	drowned	drowned	speak	spoke	spoken
eat	ate	eaten	steal	stole	stolen
fly	flew	flown	swim	swam	swum
give	gave	given	swing	swung	swung
go	went	gone	take	took	taken
grow	grew	grown	tear	tore	torn
hide	hid	hidden/hid	throw	threw	thrown
know	knew	known	wake	woke/waked	waked
lay	laid	laid	wear	wore	worn

Sensory Words: Describing Objects

Size/Weight

enormous

gigantic

huge

immense

light

minute

tiny

towering

Shape

crooked

curved

deep

many-sided

oblong

pointed

round

shallow

square

Color

bright

colorful

dark

dazzling

flaming

flickering

glaring

glowing

multi-colored

pale

radiant

shining

shiny

Texture

bumpy

cold

cool

crinkled

cuddly

damp

dry

fluffy

furry

gooey

greasy

hairy

hard

hot

icy

jagged

lukewarm

moist

muddy

oily

prickly

rough

rippling

rubbery

shaggy

sharp

silky

slimy

slippery

slushy

smooth

soft

sticky

uneven

velvety

warm

wet

Sound

buzzing

clanging

hissing

humming

popping

ringing

screeching

sizzling

slacking

slushing

squawking

thumping

thudding

tinkling

Odor

clean

fresh

musty

smoky

strong

sweet

Sensory Words: Describing Food

Shape	Taste	Texture	Odor
circle	bitter	cold	fishy
diamond	bland	crisp	fresh
oval	burnt	dry	meaty
rectangle	buttery	gooey	savory
round	creamy	gritty	smoky
square	delicious	hard	sour
triangular	fishy	hot	stinky
	flavorful	icy	strong
	fruity	moist	sweet
	hot	oily	
	juicy	smooth	
	mild	soft	
	nutty	sticky	
	peppery	waxy	
	salty		
	smooth		
	sour		
	spicy		
	strong		
	sugary		
	tasteless		
	tasty		

Sensory Words:
Describing Animals and People

Eyes

beady

black

blue

bright

brilliant

brown

clear

dark

dazzling

dreamy

dull

enormous

expressive

flashy

flaming

glaring

glowing

gray

hazel

large

laughing

oval

radiant

sparkling

starry

wide

Ears

droopy

floppy

huge

pointed

rounded

small

miniature

Body Build

big

bulky

chubby

colossal

enormous

gigantic

heavy

huge

large

light

little

long

minute

petite

short

skinny

small

stout

tall

thin

tiny

towering

Tail

curled

chopped

chubby

flat

long

short

stubby

thin

Hair/Body Covering

bald

black

blonde

brown

brunette

coarse

crinkled

curly

dark

feathered

fluffy

golden

gray

green

long

red

scaly

short

smooth

spotted

straight

thick

white

yellow

Complexion

blushing

dark

light

pale

radiant

rosy

tan

wrinkled

Sounds

bark

bleat

cackle

coo

cry

groan

growl

hoot

howl

hiss

peep

purr

scream

screech

snarl

snort

tweet

wail

whine

Personality

bold

ferocious

fierce

generous

gentle

happy

mean

shy

vicious

Sensory Words: Describing Settings

Weather	Sounds			Odors
breezy	babbling	jingling	swishing	
cold	banging	lapping	thud	
cool	bellowing	loud	thumping	
damp	blaring	noisy	thundering	
dusty	blasting	patter	tinkling	
dry	booming	popping	whimpering	
foggy	bumping	quiet	whispering	
frosty	buzzing	raging	whistling	
hazy	cheering	raspy	working	
hot	chiming	ringing	yelling	
humid	clanging	roaring		
murky	clapping	rowdy		
rainy	crackling	rumbling		**Odors**
starry	crashing	rustling		smoky
stormy	crunching	screeching		clean
sunny	deafening	shrill		fresh
warm	echoing	silence		moldy
wet	exploding	sizzling		musty
windy	gurgling	sloshing		rotten
	hissing	snapping		smoky
	howling	splashing		stale
	humming	squeaking		strong
		still		sweet

Words That Express Emotions

Happiness or Pleasure

glad	amused	comfortable	enthralled
peaceful	thrilled	joyful	delighted
cheerful	proud	excited	ecstatic
satisfied	pleased	contented	courageous

Sadness or Apprehension

unhappy	lonely	tearful	nervous
disappointed	gloomy	upset	frightened
discouraged	sorrowful	troubled	fearful
hopeless	angry	miserable	anxious
pathetic	serious		

Amusement

silly	loony	funny	jovial
comical	jolly	ridiculous	hilarious

Loving and Caring

liking	kind	helpful	true
friendly	generous	fond	pleasant

Synonyms

ability—power, capability, energy, force, might

about—concerning, regarding, relating to, referring to dealing with

accomplish—do, achieve, attain, fulfill

ache—pain, affliction, agony, distress, misery

add—join, unite, accompany, associate, combine

advise—teach, direct, educate, inform, train, tutor, suggest

alarm—surprise, astound, amaze, astonish, bewilder, startle

almost—about, nearly

apply—utilize, use, employ, operate

ask—question, request, inquire

attractive—lovely, beautiful, captivating

automobile—car, vehicle

awkward—clumsy, bungling, inept, rough

bad—naughty, evil, wicked, villainous

bare—empty, vacant, barren, cold

battle—fight, encounter, brawl, contest, encounter, quarrel

before—prior to, previous, prior

begin—start, commence, originate

beneath—under, below, underneath

big—large, enormous, gigantic, great, huge, mighty

bold—valiant, brave, courageous, daring, fearless, heroic

boy—lad, guy, youth, fellow, youngster

brilliant—bright, clear, gleaming, radiant, shimmering

build—construct, erect, make, put up, manufacture

call—summon, command, cry, address, demand, exclaim, proclaim, shout

calm—mild, gentle, mellow, soothing, placid, cool, peaceful, quiet, serene

capture—apprehend, catch, take, trap

caring—kind, gentle, benevolent, amiable, loving

carry—bring, lug, transport, convey, support

Synonyms *(cont.)*

certain—sure, unquestionable, inevitable, undeniable, definite

change—alter, substitute, modify, vary, transform

charming—delightful, elegant, enchanting

children—youngsters, juveniles

close—shut, seal

colossal—huge, vast, enormous, immense, gigantic, tremendous

comfort—ease, assist, console, encourage

companion—friend, buddy, pal, ally, comrade

completion—finish, finalé, conclusion, termination

conceited—vain, empty, frivolous, hollow

conclusion—end, finish, conclude, completion, termination

correct—right, honest, just, accurate, valid, proper

creek—brook, stream, rivulet

crowd—push, shove, force, jostle

delicious—tasty, flavorful, zestful, savory

demonstrate—show, display, exhibit

develop—grow, mature, develop, expand, increase

devour—eat, consume, gobble

disregard—ignore, pass over, take no account of

durable—hard, rigid, compact, firm, solid, strong

during—while, simultaneously

empire—nation, country, community, realm, kingdom

enough—sufficient, adequate, ample, plenty

error—mistake, blunder, failure, fault, misconception, oversight

evil—wicked, corrupt, vile

fast—quick, rapid, brisk, hasty, swift

find—discover, uncover, come across, run across, stumble upon

firm—tough, hardy, strong, sturdy

food—nourishment, sustenance

fragment—part, portion, allotment, bit, piece, scrap

Synonyms *(cont.)*

frequently—often, generally, repeatedly, oftentimes

give—grant, provide, furnish, present, supply

glen—hollow, valley

globe—world, earth

good—suitable, honest, reliable, worthy, righteous

got—became, received

grand—great, huge, enormous, large, vast

have—possess, control, obtain, own

help—assist, aid, encourage, facilitate

idea—concept, belief, impression, opinion, thought

keep on—resume, continue

know—realize, understand, comprehend

last—final, end

learn—understand, acquire, determine, ascertain

let—allow, permit, tolerate

like—comparable, equal, related

long—extended, lengthy, lasting, prolonged

look—appear to, seem

neat—orderly, clear, exact, precise, spotless, tidy

new—recent, fresh, strange, unfamiliar, untried

next—after, following, proceeding

now—presently, currently

ocean—sea

old—aged, ancient, antique, elderly, obsolete

picture—design, drawing, facsimile, illustration, likeness, photo, portrait

plan—devise, invent, map, prepare

play—romp, skip, frolic, perform, imagine

put—set, deposit, install, place

reply—answer, respond, acknowledge

right—correct

Synonyms *(cont.)*

say—state, affirm, allege, assert, declare, express

slender—thin, gaunt, slim

small—little, elfin, petite, slight, tiny, wee

spot—place, abode, home, area, locality

stop—halt, cease, interrupt, hinder

story—fable, tale, legend, fantasy

strange—odd, rare, unusual, unknown, uncommon

stretchable—elastic, flexible, pliable

strong—sturdy, athletic, durable, enduring, solid, tough

study—examine, investigate, scrutinize, contemplate

stupid—dumb, brainless, dense, dull, senseless

tall—lofty, high, elevated, towering

tell—relate, describe, narrate, notify, report, declare, express, say, speak, reveal

think—imagine, consider, picture, contemplate, determine, reflect, suppose, believe

time—period, date, era, season

top—summit, peak, crest, cap, pinnacle

trapped—cornered, captured, seduced

troubled—worried, anxious, apprehensive

try—endeavor, attempt

use—utilize, apply, employ, operate

very—greatly, enormously, extremely, immensely, intensely, unusually, immeasurably, exceedingly, truly, infinitely, incredibly, fully, mightily, especially

walking—strolling, wandering

want—desire, aspire, covet, crave, long for, wish

weird—strange, unusual, unique

work—labor, accomplishment, action, achievement, task, job, profession

worry—anxiety, apprehension, concern, troubled

write—record, compose, correspond, draft, scribble

zero—nothing, blank, naught, nil, nonentity

Common Synonyms and Related Words

Go	Make	"Do"	
arrive	blend	bring	sew
chase	build	buy	shave
crawl	carve	capture	shop
enter	color	carry	start
fall	copy	collect	steer
float	cut	cover	strike
fly	draw	discover	teach
glide	fix	earn	trick
hop	form	end	win
jump	mix	escape	work
leap	mold	fill	
leave	pour	frighten	
plunge	repair	hide	
ride	stir	hold	
run	stuff	know	
skip	tear	lead	
slide		left	
soar		lose	
spin		move	
travel		open	
tumble		own	
twirl		pick	
walk		play	
		quit	
		reach	
		receive	
		remove	
		seize	

Student Writer's Notebook

Antonyms

aunt - uncle
back - front
good - bad
big - little
black - white
boy - girl
brother - sister
clean - dirty
come - go
cold - hot
close - open
dark - light
daughter - son
down - up
dry - wet
fast - slow
fat - thin
father - mother
float - sink
from - to
give - take
go - stop

happy - sad
hard - soft
heavy - light
high - low
huge - tiny
in - out
large - small
left - right
long - short
loose - tight
lose - win
mine - yours
new - old
night - day
noisy - quiet
off - on
old - young
over - under
pretty - ugly
right - wrong
rough - smooth
short - tall

Homophones

ant - aunt	meat - meet
ate - eight	night - knight
be - bee	one - won
buy - by - bye	peace - piece
capital - capitol	plain - plane
cent - sent - scent	principal - principle
sight - site - cite	rain - reign
dear - deer	right - write - rite
do - due	road - rode
flea - flee	role - roll
flew - flu - flue	sail - sale
for - four	sea - see
heal - heel	some - sum
hear - here	son - sun
hole - whole	tail - tale
hour - our	toe - tow
in - inn	their - there - they're
knew - new - gnu	to - too - two
knot - not	weak - week
mail - male	wood - would

Idioms

An *idiom* is an expression that means something different from what is actually said.

Below are many idioms that are commonly used in the English language. In the second column you will find their meanings. As you think of more, add them to this list:

Idioms	Meanings
a piece of cake	very easy
turn over a new leaf	start again
spill the beans	tell a secret
hold your horses	wait
hit the ceiling	become very angry
see eye to eye	agree
in a pickle	having a hard time
for the birds	silly or useless
going to the dogs	falling apart
in one ear and out the other	hearing, but not paying attention
crocodile tears	fake tears
raining cats and dogs	raining very hard
got a bone to pick	not in agreement

_____   _____

_____   _____

_____   _____

_____   _____

_____   _____

_____   _____

Similes

Similes are used by writers to compare two unlike things. A simile likens one thing to another. Using similes in writing helps you, the writer, create clear pictures in the mind of the reader.

A simile is introduced by using one of the following words:

- **As:** This assignment is as easy as pie.

- **Like:** A happy heart is like good medicine.

- **It reminds me of:** It reminds me of my teddy bear when I was little.

- **It seemed as though:** It seemed as though there were ants in my pants.

- **I thought of:** I thought of the way it was when I was in third grade.

Use Similes to . . .

- create a quick picture or make your writing clearer.

- write a shorter paragraph and describe things more clearly.

- set the mood for each scene.

- make a picture in your mind of your characters and setting.

Student Writer's Notebook

Similes (cont.)

Here is a list of common similes. Use these in your writing to add interest and description.

blind as a bat	playful as a kitten
cheap as dirt	pleased as punch
clean as a whistle	pretty as a picture
cold as ice	round as a ball
easy as pie	sharp as a tack
free as the breeze	sick as a dog
gentle as a lamb	sly as a fox
good as gold	smart as a whip
green as grass	stubborn as a mule
hard as nails	sweet as sugar
light as a feather	thin as a rail
neat as a pin	warm as toast

Subject/Predicate

To write well, you must include a subject and a predicate in each sentence.

Subject

The *subject* tells *who* or *what* the sentence is all about. A *simple subject* tells about one person or thing. A compound sentence tells about more than one person or thing.

Below are examples of simple and compound subjects. Using both types of sentences will enrich your writing.

Simple Subject

Sally plays the tuba. (Sally is the person about whom the sentence is written. Sally is a simple subject because she is one person.)

Compound Subject

Drawing and riding bikes are my favorite hobbies. (The phrase *drawing and riding bikes* is a compound subject because it names more than one thing.)

Predicate

The predicate is the part of a sentence that tells what the subject does. The predicate always contains a verb. There are simple predicates and compound predicates, as well.

Simple Predicate

The zebra was hiding in the cage. (The words *was hiding in the cage* tell what the zebra did).

Compound Predicate

The zebra leaped and ran through the tall grass. (The words *leaped and ran through the grass* are a compound predicate because they tell about two things the subject did).

Types of Sentences

There are four different types of sentences with which you need to be familiar. Using a variety of sentences will make your writing interesting and more informative. Use the guide below to help you prepare different types of sentences.

Statement

A statement is a sentence that tells something. A statement always ends with a period.

Question

A question is a sentence that asks something. A question always ends with a question mark.

Exclamation

An exclamation is a sentence that shows strong feelings. They always end with exclamation marks.

Command

A command is a sentence that tells someone what to do. A command ends with a period or an exclamation mark.

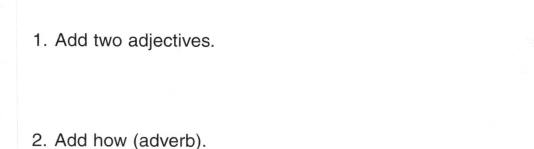

Patterns for Sentence Expansion

To make a basic sentence stronger:

1. Add two adjectives.

2. Add how (adverb).

3. Add where (prepositional phrase).

4. Add when (prepositional phrase).

5. Add why.

6. Use as many synonyms for words as possible.

Student Writer's Notebook

A nonfiction reading & writing program • A nonfiction reading & writing program

Ways to Begin a Sentence

There are many different ways to begin a sentence. Here are some of the best.

Examples:

The boys ride bikes.

1. **using two adjectives**

   Two, tough boys ride bikes.

   Loud and noisy boys ride bikes.

2. **using a question**

   Who are those loud, noisy boys riding bikes down the road?

3. **using a prepositional phrase**

   In the middle of the road, two noisy, loud boys rode bikes.

Prepositions

about	beyond
above	down
after	during
along	for
around	in
at	into
before	of
behind	to
below	toward
beside	under

4. **using an interjection**

   Wow! Those boys are loud and noisy!

Sentence Starters

The following words are useful for beginning sentences. Add others you discover to the list.

- after
- as
- before
- during
- finally
- if
- instead of
- last night
- on the way to
- rather than
- since
- suddenly
- this afternoon (morning, evening)
- yesterday
- when
- while

Student Writer's Notebook

A nonfiction reading & writing program • *A nonfiction reading & writing program*

How to Construct a Paragraph

When you write a paragraph, it is important that you explain ideas clearly so that your reader understands and can see a picture of what you are writing. Every paragraph should have a topic sentence, three supporting sentences, and a concluding sentence.

1. Choose a topic.

2. Write a topic sentence to introduce the subject of your paragraph.

3. Provide supporting details about the subject, each in its own sentence. Remember, there must be at least three supporting sentences per paragraph.

4. Write a concluding sentence. Use the ideas below to help you:

    - Repeat the topic sentence.

    - Write the topic sentence in a different way.

    - Use an exclamation sentence to show emotion about the past three sentences.

    - Give a personal opinion of the last three sentences.

5. Write a title that clearly states about what you are writing.

Student Writer's Notebook

A nonfiction reading & writing program • A nonfiction reading & writing program

Directions for Writing Quotations

To write quotation marks in your writing, follow these guidelines.

1. Make sure all words of a speaker are inside quotation marks.

2. Start a new paragraph each time a new person begins to speak.

3. Finish the words of the speaker with a comma, question mark, or exclamation mark before the final quotation mark. If the speaker's words come at the end of a sentence, place the punctuation (period, question mark, exclamation point) and then use quotation marks.

4. It is usually a good idea to use said or a synonym of said and the name of the person speaking before or after the quote.

Examples:

Statements:

Mara said, "I want to play tetherball."

"I think I would like to go to recess," stated Travis.

Questions:

"Can I have a snack?" asked José.

Stephanie asked, "How many can I have?"

Exclamations:

"I can't come to the party!" groaned Nancy.

Amber grumbled, "I got only three gifts from my grandma!"

Synonyms for Said

added	exclaimed	nagged	shrieked
agreed	giggled	ordered	snapped
argued	grinned	pleaded	sobbed
asked	grunted	pointed out	spoke
babbled	insisted	prayed	sputtered
began	instructed	questioned	stated
boasted	laughed	remarked	thought
called	lectured	repeated	wailed
commanded	lied	replied	whined
complained	mentioned	roared	whispered
cried	moaned	ruled	
decided	mumbled	scolded	
described	murmured	screamed	

Structure of a Good Story

Opening (Beginning)

- Write an exciting topic sentence.
- Present the main characters.
- Identify the setting.
- Introduce the problem (if there is one).

Middle

- Introduce other characters
- Discuss the problem in more detail.
- Write about ways to solve the problem.
- Write actions that lead to the climax (the most exciting part of the story).

Conclusion (End)

- This is the part that brings all the parts together to create a solution to the problem. This part includes the final details of the story, bringing it to a close.

Climax (Solution)

- This is the most exciting part of the story.
- The writer shows how the characters' problems were solved.

Dialogue: When to Write It

Dialogue is what your characters say to each other. It is very important to stories for the following reasons:

1. **Dialogue helps the reader know and understand the characters in the story.** You can tell a lot about the characters by the things they say.

   Example: "That is a really ugly art project you made!" stated Amber.

   "I really like your picture. I think you deserved to win!" whispered Ashley.

   Both friends gave their opinions of the artwork. Which one was really your friend?

2. **Dialogue can tell a reader about events that have happened before.**

   "I was just thinking, Jessica."

   "What about?"

   "Oh, I was just thinking about when we dressed up in mom's dresses and had a tea party for my birthday," stated Ashley.

3. **Dialogue gives the readers clues about what will happen in the future.**

   "Go to Big Bear with us. It will be so much fun!"

   "All right, I'll go, but I won't go for a ride in the boat. I don't do boats."

   "That's right. You nearly fell into the water last time you rode with your friend."

4. **Dialogue is an important part of moving your story in a forward direction.** Your characters can take the readers along.

   "Really, Glenn, you didn't do too badly on your homework assignment."

   "He's right, you should have seen Randy's homework grade!"

   "Oh, that reminds me, we'd better catch up to Randy. He is waiting for us!"

To improve your dialogue writing, practice the following ideas:

1. **Listen**

   Everywhere you go listen to how people talk to each other. Listen to your friends, teachers, little kids, people in the theaters, at parks, and in stores. Listen to the way they express themselves, their languages, and their accents. This will give you a lot of great ideas for writing.

2. **Visualize** (make pictures in your mind)

   When you write dialogue, imagine your characters walking around speaking to each other. Write the words you think they would really say.

3. **Make it Count**

   The words that your characters say should be meaningful and add to the ideas in your story. They can be useful for giving clues, moving to new scenes, giving information about other characters, or telling information about themselves and how they think, feel, and act.

Dialogue: How to Write It

Make sure the exact words the character says are inside the quotation marks.

Example:

Tanya said, " *I want to go to the ice cream store now.*"

"*I want to go to Dairy Queen now,*" said Tanya, "*because it will close soon.*"

"*I want to go to Dairy Queen.*" Tanya stood up. "*It will be too late soon!*"

In the above examples, Tanya said almost the exact same thing but in different ways.

The quotations go around what she says and nothing else.

The words *Tanya said,* tell who is speaking. These are called explanatory words.

Make sure to separate the explanatory words from what is being said with a comma or commas except when a new sentence is beginning.

In the second example above, there are commas after the word *now* and after the explanatory words *said Tanya* because *I want to go to Dairy Queen now because it is going to close* is one complete sentence.

In the third example above, there is a period after the word *Queen* because Tanya begins a new sentence.

Do not capitalize the second part of a quoted sentence, as show below:

"*I really would like to win that prize,*" yelled Timothy, "*but I lost the lucky ticket!*"

The word *but* is not capitalized because it is part of the sentence, *I really would like to win that prize, but I lost my lucky ticket!*

Point of View

A person who writes fiction writes with a certain voice. The writer takes a stand on an issue that he or she is presenting. The writer makes the characters and situation come alive. The place the writer chooses to speak from is called the *point of view*. The point of view that an author of a novel uses is usually one of these shown below:

First Person/Third Person

❏ **A story told from the first person point of view is an *I* story.** One of the characters in the story tells it as he or she sees it. This character might be a hero or heroine of the story. The feelings, personality, fears, hopes, frustrations, and things that motivate the character are shown to the reader through his or her writings.

❏ **A story told from the third person point of view is a *he* or *she* story.** In the third person point of view, the writer still tells the story from the character's view, but the character is referred to as he or she. We will still understand and read how the character thinks and feels, but the writing will read "he thought" or "she thought."

Style

Style is the way the writer writes the story. It is the kinds of words that the writer chooses and the way these words are put into sentences for the reader. Style is how the writer uses language. It is what makes each writer different from another and one story different from another.

Below are some examples of different writing styles.

First Lines of Stories

1. Long ago, in a land far away, lived a beautiful princess.

2. "Hey, you!" yelled the old man. "What are you doing in my back yard?"

3. The night was dark and stormy. Spiders were hung on the walls. All the tables were covered in black paper. It was the perfect night for a Halloween party!

4. The little alien tiptoed quietly into the schoolroom. He hoped no one would notice his new shoes.

5. Sarah jumped up from her bed. She thought she saw a shadow on the wall. Where was her favorite teddy bear?

Extension Activity: Choose your very favorite style. Write a one-page story that begins with one of the sentence starters above. When you are finished, publish your story and share it with your classmates.

Dead Words

Some words in the English language are used too often. This makes them become powerless. They are called *dead words*. Below is a list of dead words. The words that follow the dead words can be used to replace them.

also—too, in addition to

awesome, cool, rad—wonderful, marvelous, fantastic, superb, excellent

scared—afraid, fearful, terrified, frightened

have to—need to, must

very—extremely, fantastically, unusually, incredibly, truly, fully, especially, mightily

like—such as, similar to

kid—child, boy, girl

mad—angry, frustrated, furious

got, get—received, obtained, succeed in

then—first, second, next, later, finally, afterward, meanwhile, soon

nice—pleasant, charming, fascinating, delightful, pleasurable, pleasing

lots—numerous, heaps, many

fun—pleasant, amusing

good—excellent, fine, marvelous, superb, wonderful

but—however, yet, still, on the other hand

awful—alarming, frightful, terrible, shocking, horrid

great—wonderful, marvelous, fantastic

guy—man, person, boy, youngster

funny—amusing, humorous, laughable

Peer Response Forms

Your name: _____

Author's name: _____

Mark an "x" under the appropriate place on the provided lines:

	very much	somewhat
1. I enjoyed reading this.		
2. This made sense to me.		
3. The writing is imaginative.		

Finish the following statements as best you can. Remember, your job is to help the writer.

1. One thing I really like about this writing is . . .

2. One thing I think the author can improve upon is . . .

3. Something I would like the author to tell more about is . . .

4. One last comment is . . .

Peer Response Forms *(cont.)*

Your name:_____

Author's name: _____

1. Check the correct box after you have proofread* for the following.
   (Write your proofreading marks on the author's paper.)

   ❏ Capitalization

   ❏ Punctuation end-marks

   ❏ Sentence run-ons and fragments

   ❏ Commas

   ❏ Quotation marks

   ❏ New paragraph indentations

   ❏ Correct spelling

   ❏ Logic (Makes sense)

2. Something I might change in this writing is . . .

3. Something I would definitely keep in this writing is . . .

*A set of proofreading marks is provided on page 59.

Student Writer's Notebook

A nonfiction reading & writing program • *A nonfiction reading & writing program*

Form for a Friendly Letter

Date _____

Dear _____ ,
      Greeting

_____

_____

_____

_____

_____

_____

_____

_____

_____

_____

_____

_____

                      _____
                      Closing: Love/Affectionately/Fondly,

                      _____
                      Signature

Student Writer's Notebook

A nonfiction reading & writing program • A nonfiction reading & writing program

Form for Addressing an Envelope

Name (Sender)
Address (Number and Street)
City, State and Zip

Stamp

Name (Recipient)
Address (Number and Street)
City, State and Zip

Form for a Business Letter

_____
Sender's street number and street name

_____
Sender's city, state and zip

_____
Date

_____
Person Receiving Letter (Recipient) name

_____
number and street name

_____
city, state and zip

Dear Sir/Madam:

_____

_____

_____

_____

_____

_____

_____

_____

_____
Closing: Yours truly/Sincerely,

_____
Signature

Comparison and Contrast Writing

When you are writing a comparison/contrast paper, it is important to follow the guidelines below.

Guidelines

1. Choose a topic.

2. Write the first paragraph describing the good points or similarities. Include examples to support your ideas.

3. Write the second paragraph describing the negative points or the differences. Also include examples.

4. Write the third paragraph summarizing paragraphs one and two.

Example:

Chicken Nuggets or Cheeseburgers?

Chicken nuggets are very different from cheeseburgers. They both taste very good and are made by fast food restaurants. Lots of people order one or the other almost every day. They can both be eaten if you are in a hurry.

Chicken nuggets, however, are much tastier than cheeseburgers. They have a juicier taste. Nuggets are generally dipped in sauce and cheeseburgers are not. Nuggets come without buns and are not messy to eat. Cheeseburgers are very messy and fall apart when you eat them.

I think that nuggets are much better because I like the taste of them. More of my friends prefer nuggets, as well. They are fun to eat and even better to dip. Nuggets are definitely the better choice for a quick snack!

Use the guidelines to help you create a fantastic comparison/contrast essay of your own.

Student Writer's Notebook

A nonfiction reading & writing program • A nonfiction reading & writing program

Cause-and-Effect Writing

When writing cause and effect papers, follow the format below.

Guidelines

1. Choose a topic.

2. Describe the incident (the cause) in paragraph one. Be sure to tell exactly what happened.

3. Describe the result or results of the cause. State each one clearly in paragraph two. Make sure the results are clearly described.

4. Suggest a solution to the effects in paragraph three, especially if they are negative.

Example:

I am Cold

I am cold today because I did not wear my jacket to school. It is rainy and I am soaked to the bone. I got drenched when I was waiting for the bus. My umbrella is still on my bed in my bedroom. The rain just keeps pouring out of the clouds.

Now I will be wet all day in school. My jeans will take a long time to dry. I will probably get sick. I will need to take medicine and mom will be unhappy. The nurse will probably have to call my mother.

I think that calling my mom would be a great idea. She could bring me some dry clothes. I would feel much better and I might not even get sick. It would nice to have dry clothes again. I think that calling Mom is the best idea I've had!

Use the guidelines to help you create a fantastic cause and effect essay of your own.

Persuasive or Editorial Writing

When writing an opinion or editorial, follow the format below:

Guidelines

1. Choose a topic for your writing.

2. Give a detailed description of the problem or issue in paragraph one.

3. In paragraph two, tell the reader why this issue or problem is important to consider or think about.

4. Write the benefits that would happen because of your solution in paragraph three.

Example:

No More Homework for 3rd Graders

There should be a law made that states children in the third grade should no longer be required to do homework. Homework is very boring. Kids should not have to do any of it at all. This issue needs to be addressed because children everywhere have homework on weeknights when they go to school.

It is very important to cancel homework for all third-grade students at this time because they are very busy with other things in life. They have friends. They have chores, clubs, and sports. Homework takes a lot of time. If third graders didn't have homework, they would be much happier students.

The best solution to this problem in the United States is to pass a law that bans homework for all third graders. Teachers need to be told they cannot give homework. There need to be police who make sure no one is getting homework in the third grade. If a person breaks the rule, they should be put in jail.

The things that would happen if there were laws to ban homework would be terrific! All third graders would have more time to play after school. They would have more time for friends. They would be happier and give their parents less trouble. Lastly, they would fight with their parents less because there would be no reason to fight with them. Let's get rid of homework!

Use the guidelines to help you create a fantastic opinion essay or editorial of your own.

Writing a Summary

Summaries are short essays that retell something. Only the most important facts about the story are written.

Example of Important Facts for *Charlotte's Web*:

The facts about Wilbur being saved from death would be most important. His friendship with Charlotte would need to be explained. Charlotte's sacrifice of her life to save Wilbur would also be very important. The summary needs to include all the things Charlotte did right and the wonderful friendship that she built with Wilbur.

When writing a summary, read the story or article very carefully. After you have taken notes on all the important issues, do the following:

1. List all the important facts in your own words.

2. Combine any facts, if it is possible.

3. Rewrite the facts as simply as possible.

_____

_____

_____

_____

_____

_____

_____

_____

_____

_____

_____

_____

_____

Conducting an Interview (Choice #1)

Here are some questions to use when interviewing someone concerning his or her career.

1. What is your whole name?

2. What is your occupation or profession?

3. Where do you work?

4. How long have you worked there?

5. When did you become interested in this occupation/profession?

6. What made you want to choose this career?

7. What are your responsibilities?

8. What is your favorite thing to do during the work day? Explain why.

9. What is your least favorite part of work? Why?

10. What kind of training was needed for this job? How long did it take?

11. Do you think you will do this job for the rest of your life? Why or why not?

Conducting an Interview (Choice #2)

This is a list of general information topics that you may use to collect data instead of using the first interview form. Use the type that works best for you.

General Interview Topics

- name

- date

- birthplace

- address

- family history (ancestors and where they came from)

- cultural background

- family

- education

- friends

- education

- work experience

- current occupation/career

- description of his or her job

- description of the workplace

- interests/hobbies

- favorites (books, shows, color, flower, season, sport, movie, family activity)

- dislikes

- memories from childhood

- belief system

Student Writer's Notebook

A nonfiction reading & writing program ° *A nonfiction reading & writing program*

Writing a Newspaper Article

Important thing to include in a newspaper article:

- Headline

- Byline

- Dateline

- Illustration (optional)

- Paragraph 1: who, what, when, and where

- Paragraph 2+: how and why, organized logically

- Last Paragraph: conclusion, summary, or future prospects

List of Headlines

(Add interesting headlines you read or write here.)

Writing a Newspaper Article (cont.)

Headline:

Byline:	Dateline:

Details	
Where?	**What?**
Who?	**Why?**
When?	**How?**

Writing a Book Report

When you write a book report, tell the important events, or plot, of the book. Don't give away the ending of the story. Explain the most important idea. Write about the main characters, the people or animals in the story, the setting, where and when the story takes place. Finally, give your opinion of the book. Make sure to explain why others should read it or why they would not be interested.

Include the following items in your book report:

Paragraph 1

title, author, illustrator, copyright, and type of literature (fiction, nonfiction, mystery, biography, autobiography, etc.)

Paragraph 2

main characters, names, how the characters look and act

Paragraph 3

tell when the story takes place and where (setting)

Paragraph 4

discuss the plot of the story, the theme, or the main idea

Paragraph 5

give your personal opinion and recommendation of the book

There are many different ways to present book reports. Add ideas you find interesting below.

Creating an Outline

Writers use outlines to organize their information for reports, articles, and other kinds of writing. The title of the outline gives the topic which will be written about. The main topics are listed after Roman numerals. The subtopics, or details about the main topics, follow capital letters. All subtopics are indented.

Title: _____

I. _____

    Main Topic (begin with a capital letter)

  A. _____

      Subtopic (begin this with a capital letter)

  B. _____

      Subtopic

  C. _____

      Subtopic

II. _____

    Main Topic

  A. _____

      Subtopic

  B. _____

      Subtopic

  C. _____

      Subtopic

Web Form

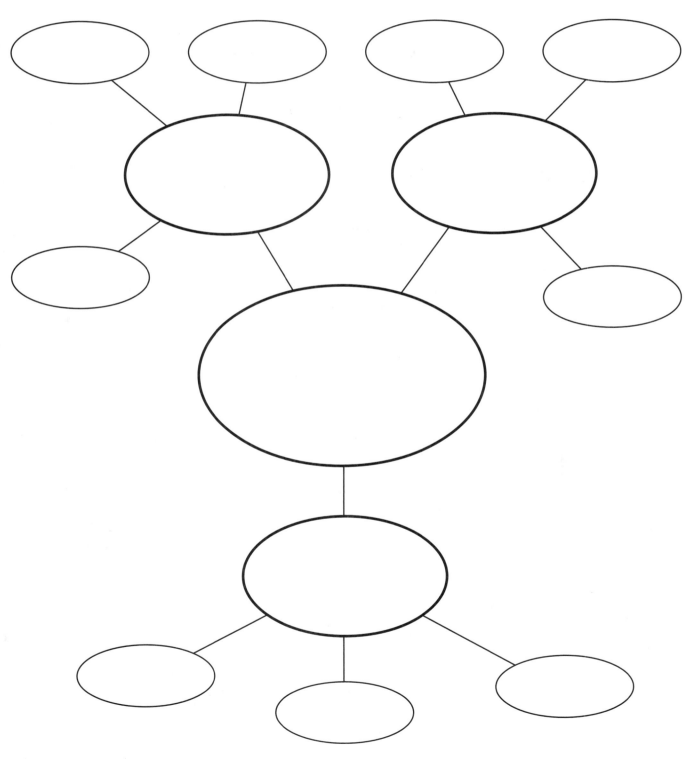

Proofreading Symbols

a ≡	capital letter
⊙	add period
	take out
A̸	lower case
∨ ∧	put in
?	does not make sense
D.W.	dead word
^,	add comma
" " ∨	add quotations
#	add a space
¶	make a new paragraph

Student Writer's Notebook

A nonfiction reading & writing program • A nonfiction reading & writing program

Editing Checklist

☐ Capitalize important words in the title.

☐ Indent paragraphs and check margins.

☐ Punctuation is correct.

☐ All sentences are complete ideas.

☐ Includes colorful speech (adjectives, adverbs, similes, synonyms).

☐ Transition words (because, since, when, while) are used.

☐ Check to make sure dead words are changed and overused words are avoided.

☐ Unnecessary words are left out.

☐ Spelling is correct.

☐ Writing is very neat and readable.

Using Writing Tools

Each profession has its own special type of tools and writing is just like all the others. The first things that every good writer needs are pencils, paper, a typewriter, or a computer. If you only have paper and pencil, you can still be a great writer. Some of the most famous books in the world have been written by hand. Below are listed some of the popular tools of the profession.

A good dictionary is very important for every writer. You will need to use the dictionary to look up correct spelling, word meaning, and to improve your writing. Some of the things you will be able to find in a dictionary include pronunciation of words; synonyms (when you are looking for the right word to use); names and dates of famous people; names and locations for different places in the world; where words came from (origins); rules for using different words; expressions which can be used in the language; and if words are proper to use in your writing.

A thesaurus helps you find the right word to describe an idea or express a feeling you have. Find a copy of *Roget's International Thesaurus*. Ask your teacher or the librarian to show you how to use the system.

A general encyclopedia is usually one of the best places to start to find information about what you are writing. Two great encyclopedias to use are *The World Book Encyclopedia* and the *Encyclopedia Britannica*.

The Internet is a great place to gain information, as well as online encyclopedias and reference materials.

The library is one of the writer's most important tools. Learn how to use the school library and the community library. Librarians can be very helpful. Don't be afraid to ask. You will receive many good suggestions.

Gathering and Organizing Information

Name _____ Date _____

General Topic Area _____

Three Subtopic Areas _____

_____

_____

Four Written Sources of Information

_____

_____

_____

_____

Subject(s) to be Interviewed _____

_____

Planned Observation(s) _____

_____

_____

_____

Source of Illustrations _____

_____

Citing Sources

It's okay to use the ideas and information that other people have written. However, if you do, you need to give credit where credit is due.

Below are guidelines for using information in your bibliography for your report:

Book Information—Author's full name, *Full title*, **Name of publisher, Date of publication.**

Hall, Katie. *Skeletons! Skeletons!* Scholastic, 1993.

Magazine Information—Author's name, "Title of the Article," *Title of the Magazine*, **Date of Publication.**

Sunquist, Fiona. "Bobcats." *National Geographic World*, 1999.

Encyclopedia—"Title of the Article," *Title of the Encyclopedia,* **Year of publication, Page numbers.**

"Maya," *The New Book of Knowledge*, 1996. pp. 184–187.

The Bibliography

The bibliography is the last page of your report! It will be very easy to write the resources if you have recorded them on a bibliography page. Make sure to follow the guidelines on the previous page. Alphabetize your bibliography.

Below is an example of a bibliography in alphabetical order.

Gordon, David. "Ice Pop." *National Geographic World*, 1998.

Hall, Katie. *Skeletons! Skeletons!* Scholastic, 1993.

"Maya," *The New Book of Knowledge*, 1996. pp. 184–187.

Sunquist, Fiona. "Bobcats." *National Geographic World*, 1999.

Bibliographies are single spaced, with one space between each entry. The first line of each entry begins at the left margin, but the second line is indented. When you write your report by hand, titles must be underlined because there are no italics. Make sure to check the correct order and punctuation. Use the guide above.